LOVE YOU NICOLA!

compiled and edited by

Deedee Cuddihy

First Published 2015
Copyright©2015 by Deedee Cuddihy

No part of this book may be
reproduced, except for short extracts
for quotation or review, without the
written permission of the publisher
(unless it's the bits that I borrowed
myself, of course . . .)

ISBN 978 0 9930986 1 1

Published by Deedee Cuddihy
10 Otago Street,
Glasgow G12 8JH
Scotland

Cover image: Kjell Nilsson-Maki
Source: cartoonStock.com

Printed by Bell and Bain ltd, Glasgow

Dedication

"Love You Nicola!" is dedicated to all those people on the internet whose marvellous words have been included in this book. And also to the late John Aitkenhead; his daughter, Val Graham; the late Margaret Ewing, MP, MSP (who was Margaret Bain when she showed me around Westminster back in the day) and the late Margo MacDonald, MP, MSP. And, of course, to Nicola Sturgeon...

Foreword

What is it about Nicola Sturgeon that inspires so much affection? Whether she's sparring with other political leaders; appearing on talk shows; attending award ceremonies; championing macaroni pies or simply going on walkabouts, she cannot put a foot wrong - even, memorably, when treading a balance beam. People love her - not just here in Scotland but all over the world, as this book demonstrates.

Nicola ... you have served us well and inspired heart in our nation again. you have worked tirelessly without doubt and along with Alex Salmond...a man whose shoes I never would have thought could have been filled by such a powerful pair of high heels

(Issy on Facebook)

scotland has its own princess she is called NICOLA

(John on Facebook)

Nicola Sturgeon's appeal is now almost above politics - straying into the kind of affection normally associated with celebrities or members of the royal family.

(journalist Iain Macwhirter commenting on the Nicola phenomenon)

Nicola Sturgeon - arguably the most famous non-fictional woman in Scottish history, always excepting Mary, Queen of Scots.

(journalist Ian Jack commenting on the Nicola phenomenon)

"She used to tease me quite a bit and cut the hair off my Barbie dolls, but apart from that Nicola was a lovely sister."

(Gillian Owens, younger sister of Nicola Sturgeon)

Nicola Sturgeon's appearance on the US Comedy Central show followed a glowing profile in the New York Times that paid tribute to Scotland feminist First Minister who "has gone from regional obscurity to one of the most powerful players in British politics".

You're a great
ambassador for us all
Nicola. We are all so
proud of you!

(Anne)

"She hugged me. I could greet!"

(a shop assistant in South Queensferry meets Nicola Sturgeon)

Nicola Sturgeon takes almost an hour to walk a few paces during a walkabout in Glasgow because she is mobbed by the adoring crowds. A speech to a sober business audience is met with whoops and cheers.

(London Evening Standard)

ACCORDING to Google, the most searched-for phrase halfway through Britain's televised election debate on April 2nd was "Nicola Sturgeon". Although unfamiliar to many English voters, the SNP chief was making light work of the leaders of the main political parties. By the end, "Can I vote for the SNP?" was also trending.

(The Economist)

*"Nicola Sturgeon
is a . . . glamorous,
power-dressing
imperatrix. "*

(Daily Mail)

Omg, Nicola Sturgeon is on the Daily Show. I love her so.

(Eliza)

Twitter's European chief, Bruce Daisley, has hailed Nicola Sturgeon as the most savvy UK politician on the social media platform. "She   is superb on Twitter" he said.

Nicola I am 62 years old and have never trusted politicians until now. You are like a breath of fresh air.

(Moira on Facebook)

Wish we had
someone like you
here in England.

(Eve on Facebook)

You spoke to my daughter for five minutes outside our house and now every time she sees your picture she says look mummy it's Nicola she's my friend. She's only three.

(Debora on Facebook)

Nicola I don't know how you do it. Never known anyone that works as hard as you. Makes one so proud to be Scottish.

(Mary)

Love this woman.
Confident my grand
child's future is in
safe hands.

(Rebecca)

Wish we had someone like you here in Bavaria.

(Ralf)

I admire you Nicola but not your politics. I so wish you were a Tory, you would be great !!

(Lindsay from Stoke-on-Trent)

Love her, the only genuine one out there trying to make the world a better place.

(mumsnet)

Want to say: thank
f*** for Nicola
Sturgeon.

(mumsnet)

Discovered that I have a weird crush on Nicola Sturgeon. In short, I probably 'wid'. Is this usual? What are your thoughts? I can't say that I ever felt the same way about Alex Salmond.

(Politics forum on Pie & Bovril website)

Woman's Hour Power List 2015: Nicola Sturgeon beats Angelina Jolie to the top spot.

"Nicola Sturgeon wields a huge amount of influence right now because of the state of both the UK union and the European one. She is the woman of the moment in terms of influence and hard power."

(BBC Radio 4)

First Minister Nicola Sturgeon was in Glasgow last night at Scotland's first LGBTI awards ceremony where she was named Politician of the Year.

And yet here she is, the brightest star in the political firmament, outshining the Westminster leaders by several million light years.

(Joan McAlpine)

According to a poll in the Daily Record, more than two thirds of Scots trust Nicola – a truly amazing achievement for any politician in this age of cynicism.

"Who does Nicola think she is to be bossing England" asks Leo McKinstry?" Its because she has bigger 8alls than dave ever will

(comment on the Daily Express website)

If Trump wins over
here, can I come over
as a political refugee?
'Cause I **love Nicola
Sturgeon**.

Gotta love it when Nicola Sturgeon completely owns everyone in First Minister's questions. Wouldn't want to mess with her.

(Kirsty)

Love you Nicola

(Alli)

I actually love her so much

(Courtney)

I still **love Nicola Sturgeon**

(Maria)

I'm so jealous that you guys have Nicola Sturgeon, I bloody love her

(Megan)

I will force u all to
love Nicola Sturgeon
in fact u may unfollow
me if u don't like her

(Ellidh)

I'm so obsessed with **Nicola Sturgeon** I **love** her so much can she take over the whole of the UK

I bloody love this woman. Such a strong leader and does it so well.

(Billie Jean)

although i'm not
scottish i do love
this lady!

(Stevie)

My modies teacher was
telling the student teacher
all about how much I **love**
Nicola Sturgeon xx

(Chloe)

Nicola Sturgeon is all over my Facebook timeline today, I proper **love** her.

(Alex)

got to love our
Nicola
Sturgeon. she's
sassy

(Stephanie)

I love Nicola Sturgeon because she isn't afraid to give George Osbourne a metaphorical happy-slap with her infinitely superior ball-sack.

(Zak)

omg I love Nicola Sturgeon??

Not sure I could **love Nicola Sturgeon** more!! "*A life without books and reading would, for me, be a life not worth living.*" *(after appearing at the Edinburgh Book Festival)*

(Rachel)

I **love** you more and more everyday! An honest, down to earth politician who says it as it is

(Alasdair)

Scotland's First Minister helps gay couple get engaged -- more reason to love nicola sturgeon

(James)

I love you so much
when can I meet you
for a selfie?!

(Marc)

EXCUSE ME!!!!!!
i **love nicola sturgeon** thx

i f***in **love Nicola sturgeon**

I actually think I
might be in **love**
with her.

(Stephen)

I absolutely love **nicola** So happy she is our First Minister

(Aimie)

I **love Nicola Sturgeon**
so much, we need
women like her in
Ireland.

(Jamie)

honestly don't think I'll ever love anybody like i love Nicola Sturgeon, like id rather have a selfie w/ her than a wain

(Sarah)

I absalutely love Nicola Sturgeon

(Katie)

Nicola Sturgeon, I love you

(Ryan)

We all wish Corbyn well.
He can be England's
Nicola Sturgeon.

I **love Nicola sturgeon** more than life itself

(David)

actually I **love Nicola Sturgeon**

(Eleanor)

I LOVE NICOLA STURGEON SO F***ING MUCH BTW!!!!!!!

So much **love** for **Nicola Sturgeon** doing her thing for Scotland, politics, women and pink blazer retailers everywhere

(Abi)

Respect the Sturg she
love the Scotland
like Sheiky

(Sheiky)

My friends having a 21st
in August, Hes a big fan
of yours, he'd love for
you to come

(Josh)

HI NICOLA I KNOW
IM ENGLISH BUT I
THINK   YOURE
AMAZING PLS LOVE
ME

(Charlotte)

You are the Nation's
Mother and all of the
people **love** you dearly.
Like all great mothers,
you are inspirational !

(David)

I'm Welsh but would love to see you as prime minister

(Tamara)

Nicola Sturgeon is a feisty woman and I **LOVE** her, she knows what's going on and she wants the best for everyone.

(Millie)

A **love Nicola Sturgeon**
more than life. some woman

(Nic)

love that Nicola Sturgeon seems more in touch with what's really happening in England than the actual Prime Minister David Cameron!

(Layla)

Love Nicola
Sturgeon so much.
Wish I was
Scottish

(Nikki)

Love Nicola Sturgeon
effortless feminism

(Prince Salman)

I actually love
nicola sturgeon
soooo much she
is a shining star
in a dark tory
sky

I'd eat cereal out her ass

(Lucy)

i'm in love with you,
always have been,
always will be...nicola
sturgeon, you are my
world x

(Brady)

I **love Nicola Sturgeon** she's such a powerful woman! She'll put Dave in his place when it comes to Scotland.

(Harvey)

Seriously, how can any red blooded men not love Nicola Sturgeon. She knows there is football tonight.

(Steve)

I'm in the U.S. On
holiday. folks at the
market today *"we love
your First Minister over
here"* Good job hen.

(Tattie Bogle)

You've got to **love** Nicola Sturgeon - "First Minister joins campaign to save the macaroni pie".

(Karen)

Nicola Sturgeon – The first
female First Minister and
sex Goddess. *My love for Nicola
Sturgeon is an unnatural and
intense one.*

(comedian Jenna Wimshurst)

Unreal how much I
love Nicola sturgeon!!!

(Collette)

my **love** for **nicola sturgeon** is fierce and eternal

(Leonie)

"I genuinely love nicola sturgeon more than a love anyone else. av never felt this way about anyone before"

(Caitlin)

I **love** watching **Nicola sturgeon** speak she doesn't take no sh**

(Alison)

Nicola: Love your shoes..!

(Trudi)

Now a typical night out
in London: -*"What do
you do?"* -"I work for the
SNP" -*"Oh my god I
LOVE Nicola Sturgeon"*

(Catriona)

**Love Nicola
sturgeon** more
than ma own
maw these days
man

(Ewan)

Nicola u are a
Scottish legend!
We all **love** u xx

(Sandra)

I actually **love** her. Every time I drive past her house, I give her a wee wave.

(Victoria)

love nicola
sturgeon so
much why is she
married and
why am i gay

OMG. I RODE THE ELEVATOR WITH HER when she was in the building for the Daily Show! I **LOVE** Nicola Sturgeon!!!

(Carter)

my friend is having her engagement gathering this Sat and would love it if you where free to attend? Will be in Glasgow

(Charlene)

nicola sturgeon "the most dangerous woman in britain" is cuttin aboot dreghorn wearin jeans. a **love** her

(Sally)

watching a documentary
about **nicola sturgeon**
and I honestly **love** her

(Anna)

Genuinely love Nicola
Sturgeon - such an
inspirational leader.

(Paul)

You've always
been so feisty! It's
what people **love**
about you. Don't
go changing!

(Janet)

A few days at my mums in England and one thing was consistent: people love Nicola Sturgeon.

(Kezia)

I hate tartain, haggas, bag pipes, highland games and the Scottish accent but still **love Nicola Sturgeon**. She could be next prime minister

(Victor)

LOVE the fact that Nicola Sturgeon is tweeting about Eurovision.

(Hollymae)

i could listen to **nicola sturgeon** talk all day
i **love** her

Shallow as this may sound, as a woman, I love Nicola Sturgeon's dress sense and style.

see you, Nicola
Sturgeon, even when
you're nippy I love you
heheh

I **LOVE NICOLA STURGEON**
SO MUCH YOU CANNOT
HAVE ANY IDEA

(Elizabeth)

Nicola Sturgeon: I've just eaten haggis. **Love** me and accept me as one of your own

(HollyBeth)

I love Nicola Sturgeon
like she's my mum

(Kaitlin)

I've never loved a bird as much as I love Nicola sturgeon

(Dean)

Pure love Nicola sturgeon

(Amy)

a actual **love nicola sturgeon** more than a **love** chicken pakora nd irn bru

(Lucy)

I'm so in love with Nicola Sturgeon that I'd happily let Scotland gain independence just so they can invade us and rule.

(Michael)

I'd f***ing **love** to see **Nicola Sturgeon** in Downing Street.

(Nick)

I think I'm still in **love** with **Nicola Sturgeon**. My partner is deeply concerned.

Nicola Sturgeon pop into my work when you're in kirkcaldy, it's KFC. I will have any meal u want sitting waiting for you, love you babe!

(Lewis)

Deedee Cuddihy is a journalist who was born and brought up in New York but has lived in Glasgow since the "Big Storm" of 1967 (which she slept through). Or was it 1968? After finishing art school in Glasgow, she realised being an artist would be too difficult - and being an art teacher would be even more difficult. So she became a journalist and has been one ever since. She is married to a Scotsman and has two grown up children - plus three granddaughters. **"Love You Nicola!"** is the 10th in her Funny Scottish Books series, the other titles including the best-selling "How to Murder a Haggis", "I Love Irn-Bru" (1 & 2), "Scottish Superstitions" and "I Love Tunnock's Tea Cakes". She loves Nicola Sturgeon.

Other titles in Deedee Cuddihy's
Funny Scottish Books series include:

"How to Murder a Haggis"

"Scottish Wedding Disasters -
and how to avoid some of them"

"Under the Skin of the Scottish
Tattoo"

"Scottish Superstitions"

"I Love Irn-Bru"

"I Love Irn-Bru 2"

"I Love Tunnocks Tea Cakes - and
lots of other biscuits"

Praise for Funny Scottish Books:

"Reading it on the bus and laughing out loud!" (Lise Winter)

"An absolute stoater!" (Viv O'Duffy)

"Hilarious!" (Murdo Morrison)

"A brilliant read!" (George Hunter)

"Lovely wee book." (Matthew Perron)

"We have found your book to be of a good quality and are flattered that you have opted to base it on our products." (letter from Tunnock's)

"Your Irn-Bru book made me smile and cheered me up." (Jonathan Kemp, director, A.G. Barr)

Deedee Cuddihy

Nothing about this can be pictured and
I wonder you garden —
DEEDEE CUDDIHY

Deedee Cuddihy

HOW TO
MURDER
A HAGGIS

Real Life Happy Horror Stories
and Burns Supper Disasters

Special Burns Night Edition

WEDDING
disasters

UNDER THE SKIN
OF
THE
SCOTTISH TATTOO

Deedee Cuddihy

SCOTTISH
SUPERSTITIONS

Deedee Cuddihy